THE UNIVERSI
WINCHE

NIGHT SKY WITH EXIT WOUNDS

NIGHT SKY WITH EXIT WOUNDS

Ocean Vuong

JONATHAN CAPE
LONDON

3 5 7 9 10 8 6 4 2

Jonathan Cape, an imprint of Vintage Publishing,
20 Vauxhall Bridge Road,
London SW1V 2SA

Jonathan Cape is part of the Penguin Random House
group of companies whose addresses can be found at
global.penguinrandomhouse.com

Penguin
Random House
UK

First published in the United States by
Copper Canyon Press, Washington, in 2016

First published in the United Kingdom by
Jonathan Cape in 2017
penguin.co.uk/vintage

A CIP catalogue record for this book is available
from the British Library

ISBN 9781911214519

Typeset in India by Thomson Digital Pvt Ltd, Noida, Delhi

Printed and bound in Great Britain by TJ International Ltd, Padstow, Cornwall

Penguin Random House is committed to a sustainable future for
our business, our readers and our planet. This book is made
from Forest Stewardship Council® certified paper.

MIX
Paper from
responsible sources
FSC® C018179

tặng mẹ [và ba tôi]

for my mother [& father]

The landscape crossed out with a pen
reappears here

Bei Dao

CONTENTS

NIGHT SKY WITH EXIT WOUNDS

THRESHOLD

In the body, where everything has a price,
   I was a beggar. On my knees,

I watched, through the keyhole, not
   the man showering, but the rain

falling through him: guitar strings snapping
   over his globed shoulders.

He was singing, which is why
   I remember it. His voice –

it filled me to the core
   like a skeleton. Even my name

knelt down inside me, asking
   to be spared.

He was singing. It is all I remember.
   For in the body, where everything has a price,

I was alive. I didn't know
   there was a better reason.

That one morning, my father would stop
   – a dark colt paused in downpour –

& listen for my clutched breath
   behind the door. I didn't know the cost

of entering a song – was to lose
   your way back.

So I entered. So I lost.
        I lost it all with my eyes

wide open.

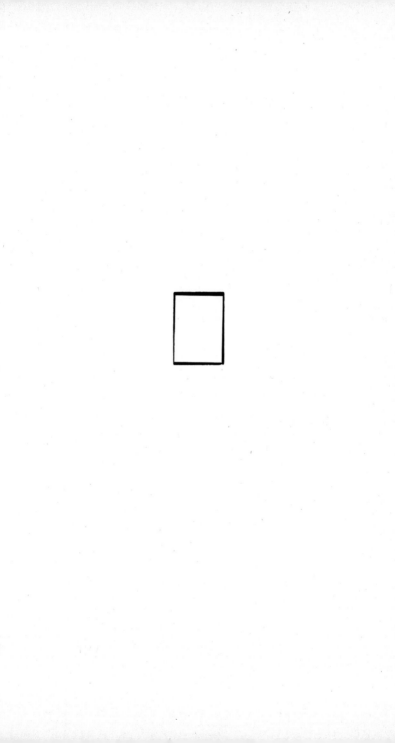

TELEMACHUS

Like any good son, I pull my father out
of the water, drag him by his hair

through white sand, his knuckles carving a trail
the waves rush in to erase. Because the city

beyond the shore is no longer
where we left it. Because the bombed

cathedral is now a cathedral
of trees. I kneel beside him to see how far

I might sink. *Do you know who I am,
Ba?* But the answer never comes. The answer

is the bullet hole in his back, brimming
with seawater. He is so still I think

he could be anyone's father, found
the way a green bottle might appear

at a boy's feet containing a year
he has never touched. I touch

his ears. No use. I turn him
over. To face it. The cathedral

in his sea-black eyes. The face
not mine – but one I will wear

to kiss all my lovers good-night:
the way I seal my father's lips

7

with my own & begin
the faithful work of drowning.

TROJAN

A finger's worth of dark from daybreak, he steps
into a red dress. A flame caught
in a mirror the width of a coffin. Steel glinting
in the back of his throat. A flash, a white
asterisk. Look
how he dances. The bruise-blue wallpaper peeling
into hooks as he twirls, his horse
-head shadow thrown on the family
portraits, glass cracking beneath
its stain. He moves like any
other fracture, revealing the briefest doors. The dress
petaling off him like the skin
of an apple. As if their swords
aren't sharpening
inside him. This horse with its human
face. This belly full of blades
& brutes. As if dancing could stop
the heart
of his murderer from beating
between his ribs. How easily a boy in a dress
the red of shut eyes
vanishes
beneath the sound of his own
galloping. How a horse will run until it breaks
into weather – into wind. How like
the wind, they will see him. They will see him
clearest
when the city burns.

AUBADE WITH BURNING CITY

South Vietnam, 29 April 1975: Armed Forces Radio played Irving Berlin's 'White Christmas' as a code to begin Operation Frequent Wind, the ultimate evacuation of American civilians and Vietnamese refugees by helicopter during the fall of Saigon.

Milkflower petals in the street
like pieces of a girl's dress.

May your days be merry and bright . . .

He fills a teacup with champagne, brings it to her lips.
Open, he says.
She opens.
Outside, a soldier spits out
his cigarette as footsteps fill the square like stones
fallen from the sky. *May
all your Christmases be white*
as the traffic guard unstraps his holster.

His fingers running the hem
of her white dress. A single candle.
Their shadows: two wicks.

A military truck speeds through the intersection, children
shrieking inside. A bicycle hurled
through a store window. When the dust rises, a black dog
lies panting in the road. Its hind legs
crushed into the shine
of a white Christmas.

On the bed stand, a sprig of magnolia expands like a secret heard
for the first time.

The treetops glisten and children listen, the chief of police
facedown in a pool of Coca-Cola.

A palm-sized photo of his father soaking
beside his left ear.

The song moving through the city like a widow.
A white . . . A white . . . I'm dreaming of a curtain of snow

falling from her shoulders.

Snow scraping against the window. Snow shredded
with gunfire. Red sky.
Snow on the tanks rolling over the city walls.
A helicopter lifting the living just

out of reach.

The city so white it is ready for ink.

The radio saying run run run.
Milkflower petals on a black dog
like pieces of a girl's dress.

May your days be merry and bright. She is saying
something neither of them can hear. The hotel rocks
beneath them. The bed a field of ice.

Don't worry, he says, as the first shell flashes
their faces, *my brothers have won the war
and tomorrow . . .*
The lights go out.
I'm dreaming. I'm dreaming . . .

to hear sleigh bells in the snow . . .

In the square below: a nun, on fire,
runs silently toward her god –

Open, he says.
She opens.

A LITTLE CLOSER TO THE EDGE

Young enough to believe nothing
will change them, they step, hand in hand,

into the bomb crater. The night full
of black teeth. His faux Rolex, weeks

from shattering against her cheek, now dims
like a miniature moon behind her hair.

In this version, the snake is headless — stilled
like a cord unraveled from the lovers' ankles.

He lifts her white cotton skirt, revealing
another hour. His hand. His hands. The syllables

inside them. O father, O foreshadow, press
into her — as the field shreds itself

with cricket cries. Show me how ruin makes a home
out of hip bones. O mother,

O minute hand, teach me
how to hold a man the way thirst

holds water. Let every river envy
our mouths. Let every kiss hit the body

like a season. Where apples thunder
the earth with red hooves. & I am your son.

IMMIGRANT HAIBUN

The road which leads me to you is safe
even when it runs into oceans.
                                    Edmond Jabès

★

Then, as if breathing, the sea swelled beneath us. If you must know anything, know that the hardest task is to live only once. That a woman on a sinking ship becomes a life raft – no matter how soft her skin. While I slept, he burned his last violin to keep my feet warm. He lay beside me and placed a word on the nape of my neck, where it melted into a bead of whiskey. Gold rust down my back. We had been sailing for months. Salt in our sentences. We had been sailing – but the edge of the world was nowhere in sight.

★

When we left it, the city was still smoldering. Otherwise it was a perfect spring morning. White hyacinths gasped in the embassy lawn. The sky was September-blue and the pigeons went on pecking at bits of bread scattered from the bombed bakery. Broken baguettes. Crushed croissants. Gutted cars. A carousel spinning its blackened horses. He said the shadow of missiles growing larger on the sidewalk looked like god playing an air piano above us. He said *There is so much I need to tell you.*

★

Stars. Or rather, the drains of heaven – waiting. Little holes. Little centuries opening just long enough for us to slip through. A machete on the deck left out to dry. My back turned to him. My feet in the eddies. He crouches beside me, his breath a misplaced weather. I let him cup a handful of the sea into my hair and wring it out. *The smallest pearls – and all for you.* I open my eyes. His face between my hands, wet as a cut. *If we make it to shore,* he says, *I will name our son after this water. I will learn to love a monster.* He smiles. A white hyphen where his lips should be. There are seagulls above us. There are hands fluttering between the constellations, trying to hold on.

★

The fog lifts. And we see it. The horizon – suddenly gone. An aqua sheen leading to the hard drop. Clean and merciful – just like he wanted. Just like the fairy tales. The one where the book closes and turns to laughter in our laps. I pull the mast to full sail. He throws my name into the air. I watch the syllables crumble into pebbles across the deck.

★

Furious roar. The sea splitting at the bow. He watches it open like a thief staring into his own heart: all bones and splintered wood. Waves rising on both sides. The ship encased in liquid walls. *Look!* he says, *I see it now!* He's jumping up and down. He's kissing the back of my wrist as he clutches the wheel. He laughs but his eyes betray him. He laughs despite knowing he has ruined every beautiful thing just to prove beauty cannot change him. And here's the kicker: there's a cork where the sunset should be. It was always there. There's a ship made from toothpicks and superglue. There's a ship in a wine bottle on the mantel in the middle of a Christmas party – eggnog spilling from red Solo cups. But we keep sailing anyway. We keep standing at the bow. A wedding-cake couple encased in glass. The water so still now. The water like air, like hours. Everyone's shouting or singing and he can't tell whether the song is for him – or the burning rooms he mistook for childhood. Everyone's dancing while a tiny man and woman are stuck inside a green bottle thinking someone is waiting at the end of their lives to say *Hey! You didn't have to go this far. Why did you go so far?* Just as a baseball bat crashes through the world.

★

If you must know anything, know that you were born because no one else was coming. The ship rocked as you swelled inside me: love's echo hardening into a boy. Sometimes I feel like an ampersand. I wake up waiting for the crush. Maybe the body is the only question an answer can't extinguish. How many kisses have we crushed to our lips in prayer – only to pick up the pieces? If you must know, the best way to understand a man is with your teeth. Once, I swallowed the rain through a whole green thunderstorm. Hours lying on my back, my girlhood open. The field everywhere beneath me. How sweet. That rain. How something that lives only to fall can be nothing but sweet. Water whittled down to intention. Intention into nourishment. Everyone can forget us – as long as you remember.

★

Summer in the mind.
God opens his other eye:
two moons in the lake.

ALWAYS & FOREVER

Open this when you need me most,
                he said, as he slid the shoe box, wrapped

in duct tape, beneath my bed. His thumb,
                still damp from the shudder between mother's

thighs, kept circling the mole above my brow.
                The devil's eye blazed between his teeth

or was he lighting a joint? It doesn't matter. Tonight
                I wake & mistake the bathwater wrung

from mother's hair for his voice. I open
                the shoe box dusted with seven winters

& here, sunk in folds of yellowed news
                -paper, lies the Colt .45 – silent & heavy

as an amputated hand. I hold the gun
                & wonder if an entry wound in the night

would make a hole wide as morning. That if
                I looked through it, I would see the end of this

sentence. Or maybe just a man kneeling
                at the boy's bed, his grey overalls reeking of
                  gasoline

& cigarettes. Maybe the day will close without
                the page turning as he wraps his arms around

the boy's milk-blue shoulders. The boy pretending
　　　　　　to be asleep as his father's clutch tightens.

The way the barrel, aimed at the sky, must tighten
　　　　　　around a bullet

to make it speak

MY FATHER WRITES FROM PRISON

Lan oi,

Em khỏe khong? Giờ em đang ở đâu? Anh nhớ em va con qua.
Hơn nữa & there are things / I can say only in the dark / how one
spring / I crushed a monarch midflight / just to know how it felt
/ to have something change / in my hands / here are those hands
/ some nights they waken when touched / by music or rather the
drops of rain / memory erases into music / hands reaching for
the scent of lilacs / in the moss-covered temple a shard / of dawn
in the eye of a dead / rat your voice on the verge of / my hands
that pressed the 9mm to the boy's / twitching cheek I was 22 the
chamber / empty I didn't know / how easy it was / to be gone
these hands / that dragged the saw through bluest 4 A.M. / cricket
screams the kapok's bark spitting / in our eyes until one or two
collapsed / the saw lodged in blue dark until one or three / started
to run from their country into / their country / the ak-47 the
lord whose voice will stop / the lilac / how to close the lilac / that
opens daily from my window / there's a lighthouse / some nights
you are the lighthouse / some nights the sea / what this means is
that I don't know / desire other than the need / to be shattered &
rebuilt / the mind forgetting / the body's crime of living / again
dear Lan or / Lan oi what does it matter / there's a man in the
next cell who begs / nightly for his mother's breast / a single drop
/ I think my eyes are like his / watching the night bleed through
/ the lighthouse night that cracked mask / I wear after too many
rifle blows / Lan oi! Lan oi! Lan oi! / I'm so hungry / a bowl of
rice / a cup of you / a single drop / my clock-worn girl / my
echo trapped in '88 / the cell's too cold tonight & there are things
/ I can say only where the monarchs / no longer come / with
wings scraping the piss-slick floor for fragments of a / phantom
woman I push my face / against a window the size of your palm
where / beyond the shore / a grey dawn lifts the hem of your
purple dress / & I ignite

HEADFIRST

Không có gì bằng cơm với cá.
Không có gì bằng má với con.
Vietnamese proverb

Don't you know? A mother's love
                              neglects pride
                    the way fire
neglects the cries
          of what it burns. My son,
                              even tomorrow
you will have today. Don't you know?
                    There are men who touch breasts
                              as they would
          the tops of skulls. Men
who carry dreams
          over mountains, the dead
                              on their backs.
But only a mother can walk
                    with the weight
of a second beating heart.
                              Stupid boy.
          You can get lost in every book
but you'll never forget yourself
                    the way god forgets
his hands.
                    When they ask you
                    where you're from,
tell them your name
          was fleshed from the toothless mouth
                    of a war-woman.

That you were not born
                    but crawled, headfirst —
into the hunger of dogs. My son, tell them
                          the body is a blade that sharpens
        by cutting.

IN NEWPORT I WATCH MY FATHER
LAY HIS CHEEK TO A BEACHED
DOLPHIN'S WET BACK

& close his eyes. His hair the shade

                              of its cracked flesh.
His right arm, inked with three falling

                              phoenixes – torches
marking the lives he had

                    or had not taken – cradles
the pinkish snout. Its teeth

                              gleaming like bullets.
Huey. Tomahawk. Semi

                              -automatic. I was static
as we sat in the Nissan, watching waves

                              brush over our breaths
when he broke for shore, hobbled

                         on his gimp leg. Mustard
-yellow North Face jacket

                    diminishing toward the grey life
smeared into ours. Shrapnel

                    -strapped. Bushwhacker. The last time
I saw him run like that, he had

                         a hammer in his fist, mother
a nail-length out of reach.

                    America. America a row of streetlights
flickering on his whiskey

                              -lips as we ran. A family
screaming down Franklin Ave.

                    ADD. PTSD. POW. Pow. Pow. Pow
says the sniper. Fuck you

                         says the father, tracers splashing
through palm leaves. Confetti

                         green, how I want you green.

Green despite the red despite

the rest. His knees sunk

in ink-black mud, he guides

a ribbon of water to the pulsing

blowhole. Ok. Okay. AK

-47. I am eleven only once

as he kneels to gather the wet refugee

into his arms. Waves

swallowing

his legs. The dolphin's eye

gasping like a newborn's

mouth. & once more

I am swinging open

the passenger door. I am running

toward a rusted horizon, running

out of a country

to run out of. I am chasing my father

the way the dead chase after

days – & although I am still

too far to hear it, I can tell,

by the way his neck tilts

to one side, as if broken,

that he is singing

my favorite song

to his empty hands.

THE GIFT

a   b   c   a   b   c   a   b   c

She doesn't know what comes after.
So we begin again:

a   b   c   a   b   c   a   b   c

But I can see the fourth letter:
a strand of black hair – unraveled
from the alphabet
& written
on her cheek.

Even now the nail salon
will not leave her: isopropyl acetate,
ethyl acetate, chloride, sodium lauryl
sulfate & sweat fuming
through her pink
I ♥ NY t-shirt.

a   b   c   a   b   c   a – the pencil snaps.

The *b* bursting its belly
as dark dust blows
through a blue-lined sky.

Don't move, she says, as she picks
a wing bone of graphite
from the yellow carcass, slides it back
between my fingers.
Again. & again

I see it: the strand of hair lifting
from her face . . . how it fell
onto the page – & lived
with no sound. Like a word.
I still hear it.

SELF-PORTRAIT AS EXIT WOUNDS

Instead, let it be the echo to every footstep
drowned out by rain, cripple the air like a name

flung onto a sinking boat, splash the kapok's bark
through rot & iron of a city trying to forget

the bones beneath its sidewalks, then through
the refugee camp sick with smoke & half-sung

hymns, a shack rusted black & lit with Bà Ngoại's
last candle, the hogs' faces we held in our hands

& mistook for brothers, let it enter a room illuminated
with snow, furnished only with laughter, Wonder Bread

& mayonnaise raised to cracked lips as testament
to a triumph no one recalls, let it brush the newborn's

flushed cheek as he's lifted in his father's arms, wreathed
with fishgut & Marlboros, everyone cheering as another

brown gook crumbles under John Wayne's M16, Vietnam
burning on the screen, let it slide through their ears,

clean, like a promise, before piercing the poster
of Michael Jackson glistening over the couch, into

the supermarket where a Hapa woman is ready
to believe every white man possessing her nose

is her father, may it sing, briefly, inside her mouth,
before laying her down between jars of tomato

& blue boxes of pasta, the deep-red apple rolling
from her palm, then into the prison cell

where her husband sits staring at the moon
until he's convinced it's the last wafer

god refused him, let it hit his jaw like a kiss
we've forgotten how to give one another, hissing

back to '68, Ha Long Bay: the sky replaced
with fire, the sky only the dead

look up to, may it reach the grandfather fucking
the pregnant farmgirl in the back of his army jeep,

his blond hair flickering in napalm-blasted wind, let it pin
him down to dust where his future daughters rise,

fingers blistered with salt & Agent Orange, let them
tear open his olive fatigues, clutch that name hanging

from his neck, that name they press to their tongues
to relearn the word *live, live, live* – but if

for nothing else, let me weave this deathbeam
the way a blind woman stitches a flap of skin back

to her daughter's ribs. Yes – let me believe I was born
to cock back this rifle, smooth & slick, like a true

Charlie, like the footsteps of ghosts misted through rain
as I lower myself between the sights – & pray

that nothing moves.

THANKSGIVING 2006

Brooklyn's too cold tonight

& all my friends are three years away.

My mother said I could be anything

I wanted – but I chose to live.

On the stoop of an old brownstone,

a cigarette flares, then fades.

I walk to it: a razor

sharpened with silence.

His jawline etched in smoke.

The mouth where I reenter

this city. Stranger, palpable

echo, here is my hand, filled with blood thin

as a widow's tears. I am ready.

I am ready to be every animal

you leave behind.

HOMEWRECKER

& this is how we danced: our mothers'
white dresses spilling from our feet, late August

turning our hands dark red. & this is how we loved:
a fifth of vodka & an afternoon in the attic, your fingers

through my hair – my hair a wildfire. We covered
our ears & your father's tantrum turned

to heartbeats. When our lips touched the day closed
into a coffin. In the museum of the heart

there are two headless people building a burning house.
There was always the shotgun above

the fireplace. Always another hour to kill – only to beg
some god to give it back. If not the attic, the car. If not

the car, the dream. If not the boy, his clothes. If not alive,
put down the phone. Because the year is a distance

we've traveled in circles. Which is to say: this is how
we danced: alone in sleeping bodies. Which is to say:

this is how we loved: a knife on the tongue turning
into a tongue.

OF THEE I SING

We made it, baby.
                      We're riding in the back of the black
limousine. They have lined
                      the road to shout our names.
They have faith in your golden hair
                      & pressed grey suit.
They have a good citizen
                      in me. I love my country.
I pretend nothing is wrong.
                      I pretend not to see the man
& his blond daughter diving
                      for cover, that you're not saying
my name & it's not coming out
                      like a slaughterhouse.
I'm not Jackie O yet
                  & there isn't a hole in your head, a brief
rainbow through a mist
                      of rust. I love my country
but who am I kidding? I'm holding
                      your still-hot thoughts in,
darling, my sweet, sweet
                      Jack. I'm reaching across the trunk
for a shard of your memory,
                      the one where we kiss & the nation
glitters. Your slumped back.
                      Your hand letting go. You're all over
the seat now, deepening
                      my fuchsia dress. But I'm a good
citizen, surrounded by Jesus

                                         & ambulances. I love
this country. The twisted faces.
                                My country. The blue sky. Black
limousine. My one white glove
                                glistening pink – with all
our American dreams.

BECAUSE IT'S SUMMER

you ride your bike to the park bruised
with 9pm the maples draped with plastic bags
shredded from days the cornfield
freshly razed & you've lied
about where you're going you're supposed
to be out with a woman you can't find
a name for but he's waiting
in the baseball field behind the dugout
flecked with newports torn condoms
he's waiting with sticky palms & mint
on his breath a cheap haircut
& his sister's levis
stench of piss rising from wet grass
it's june after all & you're young
until september he looks different
from his picture but it doesn't matter
because you kissed your mother
on the cheek before coming
this far because the fly's dark slit is enough
to speak through the zipper a thin scream
where you plant your mouth
to hear the sound of birds
hitting water snap of elastic
waistbands four hands quickening
into dozens: a swarm of want you wear
like a bridal veil but you don't
deserve it: the boy &
his loneliness the boy who finds you
beautiful only because you're not
a mirror because you don't have
enough faces to abandon you've come
this far to be no one & it's june
until morning you're young until a pop song

plays in a dead kid's room water spilling in
from every corner of summer & you want
to tell him *it's okay* that the night is also a grave
we climb out of but he's already fixing
his collar the cornfield a cruelty steaming
with manure you smear your neck with
lipstick you dress with shaky hands
you say *thank you thank you thank you*
because you haven't learned the purpose
of *forgive me* because that's what you say
when a stranger steps out of summer
& offers you another hour to live

INTO THE BREACH

The only motive that there ever was was to . . . keep them with me as long as possible, even if it meant just keeping a part of them.

Jeffrey Dahmer

I pull into the field & cut the engine.

                    It's simple: I just don't know
                    how to love a man

gently. Tenderness
a thing to be beaten

                    into. Fireflies strung
                    through sapphired air.

You're so quiet you're almost

                    tomorrow.

The body was made soft
to keep us

                    from loneliness.
                    You said that

as if the car were filling

                    with river water.

Don't worry.
There's no water.

                Only your eyes

closing.
My tongue

                in the crux of your chest.
                Little black hairs

like the legs
of vanished insects.

                I never wanted

the flesh.
How it never fails

                to fail
                so accurately.

But what if I broke through
the skin's thin page

                anyway
                & found the heart

not the size of a fist
but your mouth opening

                to the width
                of Jerusalem. What then?

To love another
man – is to leave

               no one behind
to forgive me.

               I want to leave
               no one behind.
To keep
& be kept.

               The way a field turns
               its secrets

into peonies.

               The way light
               keeps its shadow

by swallowing it.

ANAPHORA AS COPING MECHANISM

Can't sleep
so you put on his grey boots – nothing else – & step
inside the rain. *Even though he's gone,* you think, *I still want
to be clean.* If only the rain were gasoline, your tongue
a lit match, & you can change without disappearing. If only
he dies the second his name becomes a tooth
in your mouth. But he doesn't. He dies when they wheel him
away & the priest ushers you out of the room, your palms
two puddles of rain. He dies as your heart beats faster,
as another war coppers the sky. He dies each night
you close your eyes & hear his slow exhale. Your fist choking
the dark. Your fist through the bathroom mirror. He dies
at the party where everyone laughs & all you want is to go
into the kitchen & make seven omelets before burning
down the house. All you want is to run into the woods & beg
the wolf to fuck you up. He dies when you wake
& it's November forever. A Hendrix record melted
on a rusted needle. He dies the morning he kisses you
for two minutes too long, when he says *Wait* followed by
I have something to say & you quickly grab your favorite
pink pillow & smother him as he cries into the soft
& darkening fabric. You hold still until he's very quiet,
until the walls dissolve & you're both standing in the crowded
    train
again. Look how it rocks you back & forth like a slow dance
seen from the distance of years. You're still a freshman. You're
    still
terrified of having only two hands. & he doesn't know your
    name yet
but he smiles anyway. His teeth reflected in the window
reflecting your lips as you mouth *Hello* – your tongue
a lit match.

SEVENTH CIRCLE OF EARTH

On 27 April 2011, a gay couple, Michael Humphrey and Clayton Capshaw, was murdered by immolation in their home in Dallas, Texas.

Dallas Voice

₁

₂

₃

---

1. As if my finger, / tracing your collarbone / behind closed doors, / was enough / to erase myself. To forget / we built this house knowing / it won't last. How / does anyone stop / regret / without cutting / off his hands? / Another torch

2. streams through / the kitchen window, / another errant dove. / It's funny. I always knew / I'd be warmest beside / my man. / But don't laugh. Understand me / when I say I burn best / when crowned / with your scent: that earth-sweat / & Old Spice I seek out each night / the days

3. refuse me. / Our faces blackening / in the photographs along the wall. / Don't laugh. Just tell me the story / again, / of the sparrows who flew from falling Rome, / their blazed wings. / How ruin nested inside each thimbled throat / & made it sing

39

4

5

6

7

---

4. until the notes threaded to this / smoke rising / from your nostrils. Speak — / until your voice is nothing / but the crackle / of charred

5. bones. But don't laugh / when these walls collapse / & only sparks / not sparrows / fly out. / When they come / to sift through these cinders — & pluck my tongue, / this fisted rose, / charcoaled & choked / from your gone

6. mouth. / Each black petal / blasted / with what's left / of our laughter. / Laughter ashed / to air / to honey to baby / darling, / look. Look how happy we are / to be no one / & still

7. American.

ON EARTH WE'RE BRIEFLY
GORGEOUS

I

Tell me it was for the hunger
& nothing less. For hunger is to give
the body what it knows

it cannot keep. That this amber light
whittled down by another war
is all that pins my hand to your chest.

I

You, drowning
     between my arms –

stay.

You, pushing your body
     into the river
only to be left
     with yourself –

stay.

I

I'll tell you how we're wrong enough to be forgiven. How one
night, after backhanding mother, then taking a chain saw to
the kitchen table, my father went to kneel in the bathroom until
we heard his muffled cries through the walls. & so I learned – that
a man in climax was the closest thing to surrender.

I

Say surrender. Say alabaster. Switchblade.
        Honeysuckle. Goldenrod. Say autumn.
Say autumn despite the green
        in your eyes. Beauty despite
daylight. Say you'd kill for it. Unbreakable dawn
        mounting in your throat.
My thrashing beneath you
        like a sparrow stunned
with falling.

I

Dusk: a blade of honey between our shadows, draining.

I

I wanted to disappear – so I opened the door to a stranger's
car. He was divorced. He was sobbing into his hands (hands
that tasted like rust). The pink breast-cancer ribbon on his key
chain swayed in the ignition. Don't we touch each other just to
prove we are still here? I was still here once. The moon, distant &
flickering, trapped itself in beads of sweat on my neck. I let the
fog spill through the cracked window & cover my fangs. When I
left, the Buick kept sitting there, a dumb bull in pasture, its eyes
searing my shadow onto the side of suburban houses. At home, I
threw myself on the bed like a torch & watched the flames gnaw
through my mother's house until the sky appeared, bloodshot &
massive. How I wanted to be that sky – to hold every flight &
fall at once.

I

Say amen. Say amend.

Say yes. Say yes

anyway.

I

In the shower, sweating under cold water, I scrubbed & scrubbed.

I

It's not too late. Our heads haloed
            with gnats & summer too early to leave
any marks. Your hand
            under my shirt as static
intensifies on the radio.
            Your other hand pointing
your daddy's revolver
            to the sky. Stars dropping one
by one in the crosshairs.
            This means I won't be
afraid if we're already
            here. Already more than skin
can hold. That a boy sleeping
            beside a boy
must make a field
            full of ticking. That to say your name
is to hear the sound of clocks

being turned back another hour
& morning
        finds our clothes
on your mother's front porch, shed
        like week-old lilies.

EURYDICE

It's more like the sound
            a doe makes
when the arrowhead
            replaces the day
with an answer
            to the rib's hollowed
hum. We saw it coming
            but kept walking through the hole
in the garden. Because the leaves
            were pure green & the fire
only a pink brushstroke
            in the distance. It's not
about the light – but how dark
            it makes you depending
on where you stand.
            Depending on where you stand
your name can sound like a full moon
            shredded in a dead doe's pelt.
Your name changed when touched
            by gravity. Gravity breaking
our kneecaps just to show us
            the sky. Why did we
keep saying *Yes* –
            even with all those birds.
Who would believe us
            now? My voice cracking
like bones inside the radio.
            Silly me. I thought love was real
& the body imaginary.
            I thought a little chord
was all it took. But here we are –

standing in the cold field
again. Him calling for the girl.
The girl beside him.
Frosted grass snapping
beneath her hooves.

UNTITLED (BLUE, GREEN, AND BROWN): OIL ON CANVAS: MARK ROTHKO: 1952

The TV said the planes have hit the buildings.
& I said *Yes* because you asked me
to stay. Maybe we pray on our knees because god
only listens when we're this close
to the devil. There is so much I want to tell you.
How my greatest accolade was to walk
across the Brooklyn Bridge
& not think of flight. How we live like water: wetting
a new tongue with no telling
what we've been through. They say the sky is blue
but I know it's black seen through too much distance.
You will always remember what you were doing
when it hurts the most. There is so much
I need to tell you – but I only earned
one life. & I took nothing. Nothing. Like a pair of teeth
at the end. The TV kept saying *The planes . . .*
The planes . . . & I stood waiting in the room
made of broken mockingbirds. Their wings throbbing
into four blurred walls. & you were there.
You were the window.

I approach a field. A black piano waits
at its center. I kneel to play
what I can. A single key. A tooth
tossed down a well. My fingers
sliding the slimy gums. Slick lips. Snout. Not
a piano – but a mare
draped in a black sheet. White mouth
sticking out like a fist. I kneel
at my beast. The sheet sunken
at her ribs. A dented piano
where rain, collected
from the night, reflects
a blue sky fallen
into the side of a horse. Blue
thumbprint pressed
from above. As if something needed
to be snuffed out, leaving
this black blossom dropped
on a field where I am only
a visitor. A word exiled
from the prayer, flickering. Wind
streaks the pale grass flat
around us – the horse & I
a watercolor hung too soon
& dripping. Green waves
surround this black rock
where I sit turning bones
to sonatas. Fingers blurred,
I play what I know
from listening to orchards
unleash their sweetest
wrongs. The dent in this
horse wide enough to live

by. Puddle of sky
on earth. As if to look down
on the dead is to look up
at my own face, trampled
by music. If I lift the sheet
I will reveal the heart huge
as a stillbirth. If I lift the sheet
I will sleep beside her
as a four-legged shadow, hoof homed
to hoof. If I close my eyes
I'm inside the piano again
& only. If I close my eyes
no one can hurt me.

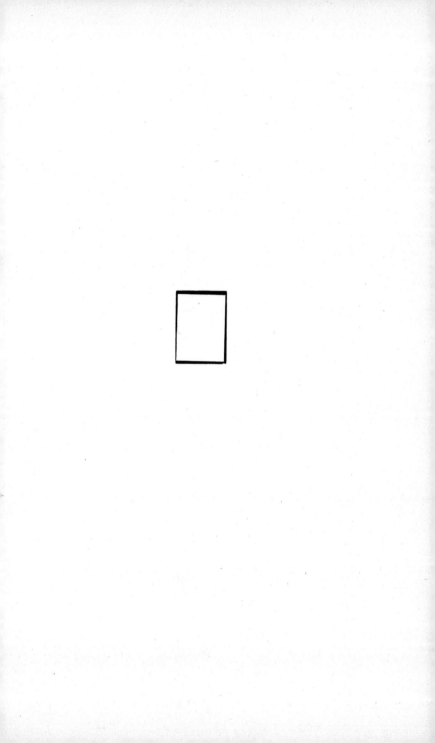

TORSO OF AIR

Suppose you do change your life.
& the body is more than

a portion of night – sealed
with bruises. Suppose you woke

& found your shadow replaced
by a black wolf. The boy, beautiful

& gone. So you take the knife to the wall
instead. You carve & carve

until a coin of light appears
& you get to look in, at last,

on happiness. The eye
staring back from the other side –

waiting.

Dearest Father, forgive me for I have seen.
Behind the wooden fence, a field lit
with summer, a man pressing a shank
to another man's throat. Steel turning to light
on sweat-slick neck. Forgive me
for not twisting this tongue into the shape
of Your name. For thinking:
this must be how every prayer
begins – the word *Please* cleaving
the wind into fragments, into what
a boy hears in his need to know
how pain blesses the body back
to its sinner. The hour suddenly
stilled. The man, his lips pressed
to the black boot. Am I wrong to love
those eyes, to see something so clear
& blue – beg to remain clear
& blue? Did my cheek twitch
when the wet shadow bloomed from his crotch
& trickled into ochre dirt? How quickly
the blade becomes You. But let me begin
again: There's a boy kneeling
in a house with every door kicked open
to summer. There's a question corroding
his tongue. A knife touching
Your finger lodged inside the throat.
Dearest Father, what becomes of the boy
no longer a boy? *Please* –
what becomes of the shepherd
when the sheep are cannibals?

TO MY FATHER / TO MY FUTURE SON

The stars are not hereditary.
Emily Dickinson

There was a door & then a door
                    surrounded by a forest.

                              Look, my eyes are not
          your eyes.

                    You move through me like rain
                                        heard
                    from another country.
Yes, you have a country.
                              Someday, they will find it
          while searching for lost ships . . .

Once, I fell in love
                    during a slow-motion car crash.

We looked so peaceful, the cigarette floating from his lips
                    as our heads whiplashed back
          into the dream & all
                              was forgiven.

          Because what you heard, or will hear, is true: I wrote
a better hour onto the page

                    & watched the fire take it back.

Something was always burning.

Do you understand? I closed my mouth
but could still taste the ash
                          because my eyes were open.

From men, I learned to praise the thickness of walls.
                              From women,
            I learned to praise.

                  If you are given my body, put it down.
If you are given anything
            be sure to leave
                          no tracks in the snow. Know

        that I never chose
which way the seasons turned. That it was always October
                              in my throat

        & you: every leaf
                    refusing to rust.

        Quick. Can you see the red dark shifting?

This means I am touching you. This means
                    you are not alone – even
            as you are not.
                          If you get there before me, if you think
                                        of nothing
& my face appears rippling
            like a torn flag – turn back.

Turn back & find the book I left
                    for us, filled
                          with all the colors of the sky
            forgotten by gravediggers.
                              Use it.

Use it to prove how the stars
                        were always what we knew

     they were: the exit wounds
                        of every
        misfired word.

DETO(NATION)

There's a joke that ends with – *huh?*
It's the bomb saying here is your father.

Now here is your father inside
your lungs. Look how lighter

the earth is – afterward.
To even write *father*

is to carve a portion of the day
out of a bomb-bright page.

There's enough light to drown in
but never enough to enter the bones

& stay. *Don't stay here*, he said, *my boy
broken by the names of flowers. Don't cry*

anymore. So I ran. I ran into the night.
The night: my shadow growing

toward my father

ODE TO MASTURBATION

because you
    were never
holy
    only beautiful
enough
    to be found

with a hook
    in your mouth
water shook
    like sparks
when they pulled
    you out

& sometimes
    your hand
is all you have
    to hold
yourself to this
    world & it's

the sound not
    the prayer
that enters
    the thunder not
the lightning
    that wakes you

in the backseat
    midnight's neon
parking lot
    holy water

smeared
     between

your thighs
     where no man
ever drowned
     from too much
thirst
     the cumshot

an art
     -iculation
of chewed stars
     so lift
the joy
     -crusted thumb

& teach
     the tongue
of unbridled
     nourishment
to be lost in
     an image

is to find within it
     a door
so close
     your eyes
& open
     reach down

with every rib
    humming
the desperation
    of unstruck
piano keys
    some call this

being human but you
    already know
it's the briefest form
    of forever yes
even the saints
    remember this the *if*

under every
    utterance
beneath
    the breath brimmed
like cherry blossoms
    foaming into no one's

springtime
    how often these lines
resemble claw marks
    of your brothers
being dragged
    away from you

you whose name
    not heard
by the ear
    but the smallest
bones
    in the graves you

who ignite the april air
    with all your petals'
here here here you
    who twist
through barbed
    -wired light

despite knowing
    how color beckons
decapitation
    i reach down
looking for you
    in american dirt

in towns with names
    like hope
celebration
    success & sweet
lips like little
    saigon

laramie money
    & sanford towns
whose trees know
    the weight of history
can bend their branches
    to breaking

lines whose roots burrow
    through stones
& hard facts
    gathering
the memory of rust
    & iron

mandibles
    & amethyst yes
touch yourself
    like this
part the softest hurt's
    unhealable

hunger
    after all
the lord cut you
    here
to remind us where
    he came

from pin this antlered
    heartbeat back
to earth
    cry out
until the dark fluents
    each faceless

beast banished
    from the ark
as you scrape the salt
    off the cock-clit
& call it
    daylight

don't
    be afraid
to be this
    luminous
to be so bright so
    empty

the bullets pass
    right through you
thinking
    they have found
the sky as you reach
    down press

a hand
    to this blood
-warm body
    like a word
being nailed
    to its meaning

& lives

NOTEBOOK FRAGMENTS

A scar's width of warmth on a worn man's neck.
    That's all I wanted to be.

Sometimes I ask for too much just to feel my mouth overflow.

Discovery: My longest pubic hair is 1.2 inches.

Good or bad?

7:18 a.m. Kevin overdosed last night. His sister left a message.
    Couldn't listen to all of it. That makes three this year.

I promise to stop soon.

Spilled orange juice all over the table this morning. Sudden
    sunlight I couldn't wipe away.

All through the night my hands were daylight.

Woke at 1 a.m and, for no reason, ran through Duffy's cornfield.
    Boxers only.

Corn was dry. I sounded like a fire,
    for no reason.

Grandma said *In the war they would grab a baby, a soldier at each
    ankle, and pull . . . Just like that.*

It's finally spring! Daffodils everywhere.
    Just like that.

There are over 13,000 unidentified body parts from the World Trade Center being stored in an underground repository in New York City.

Good or bad?

Shouldn't heaven be superheavy by now?

Maybe the rain is 'sweet' because it falls
        through so much of the world.

Even sweetness can scratch the throat, so stir the sugar well. – Grandma

4:37 a.m. How come depression makes me feel more alive?

Life is funny.

Note to self: If a guy tells you his favorite poet is Jack Kerouac,
        there's a very good chance he's a douchebag.

Note to self: If Orpheus were a woman I wouldn't be stuck
        down here.

Why do all my books leave me empty-handed?

In Vietnamese, the word for grenade is 'bom', from the French
        'pomme', meaning 'apple'.

Or was it American for 'bomb'?

Woke up screaming with no sound. The room filling with a bluish
        water called dawn. Went to kiss grandma on the forehead

just in case.

An American soldier fucked a Vietnamese farmgirl. Thus my mother exists. Thus I exist. Thus no bombs = no family = no me.

Yikes.

9:47 a.m. Jerked off four times already. My arm kills.

Eggplant = cà pháo = 'grenade tomato'. Thus nourishment
        defined by extinction.

I met a man tonight. A high school English teacher
        from the next town. A small town. Maybe

I shouldn't have, but he had the hands
        of someone I used to know. Someone I was used to.

The way they formed brief churches
        over the table as he searched for the right words.

I met a man, not you. In his room the Bibles shook on the shelf
        from candlelight. His scrotum a bruised fruit. I kissed it

lightly, the way one might kiss a grenade
        before hurling it into the night's mouth.

Maybe the tongue is also a key.

Yikes.

I could eat you he said, brushing my cheek with his knuckles.

I think I love my mom very much.

Some grenades explode with a vision of white flowers.

Baby's breath blooming in a darkened sky, across
        my chest.

Maybe the tongue is also a pin.

I'm gonna lose it when Whitney Houston dies.

I met a man. I promise to stop.

A pillaged village is a fine example of perfect rhyme. He said that.

He was white. Or maybe, I was just beside myself, next to him.

Either way, I forgot his name by heart.

I wonder what it feels like to move at the speed of thirst — if it's
        fast as lying on the kitchen floor with the lights off.

(Kristopher)

6:24 a.m. Greyhound station. One-way ticket to New York
        City: $36.75.

6:57 a.m. I love you, mom.

When the prison guards burned his manuscripts, Nguyễn
        Chí Thiện couldn't stop laughing — the 283 poems
        already inside him.

I dreamed I walked barefoot all the way to your house in the
        snow. Everything was the blue of smudged ink

and you were still alive. There was even a light the shade of
        sunrise inside your window.

God must be a season, grandma said, looking out at the blizzard
        drowning her garden.

My footsteps on the sidewalk were the smallest flights.

Dear god, if you *are* a season, let it be the one I passed through
        to get here.

Here. That's all I wanted to be.

I promise.

THE SMALLEST MEASURE

Behind the fallen oak,
the Winchester rattles
                  in a boy's early hands.

A copper beard grazes
his ear. *Go ahead.*
                  She's all yours . . .

Heavy with summer, I
am the doe whose one hoof cocks
                  like a question ready to open

roots. & like any god
-forsaken thing, I want nothing more
                  than my breaths. To lift

this snout, carved
from centuries of hunger, toward the next
                  low peach bruising

in the season's clutch.
Go ahead, the voice thicker
                  now, *drive her*

home. But the boy is crying
into the carcass of a tree – cheeks smeared
                  with snot & chipped bark.

Once, I came near
enough to a man to smell
                  a woman's scent

in his quiet praying –
as some will do before raising
                    their weapons closer

            to the sky. But through the grained mist
that makes this morning's minutes,
                    this smallest measure

            of distance, I see two arms unhinging
the rifle from the boy's grip,   .
                    its metallic shine

            sharpened through wet leaves.
I see the rifle . . . the rifle coming
                    down, then gone. I see

            an orange cap touching
an orange cap. No, a man
                    bending over his son

            the way the hunted,
for centuries, must bend
                    over its own reflection

            to drink.

DAILY BREAD

Cú Chi, Vietnam

Red is only black remembering.
Early dark & the baker wakes
to press what's left of the year
into flour & water. Or rather,
he's reshaping the curve of her pale calf
atmosphered by a landmine left over
from the war he can't recall. A fistful
of hay & the oven scarlets. Alfalfa.
Forsythia. Foxglove. Bubbling
dough. When it's done, he'll tear open
the yeasty steam only to find
his palms – the same
as when he was young. When heaviness
was not measured by weight
but distance. He'll climb
the spiral staircase & call her name.
He'll imagine the softness of bread
as he peels back the wool blanket, raises
her phantom limb to his lips as each kiss
dissolves down her air-light ankles.
& he will never see the pleasure
this brings to her face. Never
her face. Because in my hurry
to make her real, make her
here, I will forget to write
a bit of light into the room.
Because my hands were always brief
& dim as my father's.
& it will start to rain. I won't
even think to put a roof over the house –
her prosthetic leg on the nightstand,
the *clack clack* as it fills to the brim. Listen,

the year is gone. I know
nothing of my country. I write things
down. I build a life & tear it apart
& the sun keeps shining. Crescent
wave. Salt-spray. Tsunami. I have
enough ink to give you the sea
but not the ships, but it's my book
& I'll say anything just to stay inside
this skin. Sassafras. Douglas fir.
Sextant & compass. Let's call this autumn
where my father sits in a $40 motel
outside Fresno, rattling from the whiskey
again. His fingers blurred
like a photograph. Marvin on the stereo
pleading *brother, brother.* & how
could I have known, that by pressing
this pen to paper, I was touching us
back from extinction? That we were more
than black ink on the bone
-white backs of angels facedown
in the blazing orchard. Ink poured
into the shape of a woman's calf. A woman
I could go back & erase & erase
but I won't. I won't tell you how
the mouth will never be honest
as its teeth. How this
bread, daily broken, dipped
in honey – & lifted
with exodus tongues, like any other
lie – is only true as your trust
in hunger. How my father, all famine
& fissure, will wake at 4 a.m.
in a windowless room & not remember
his legs. *Go head, baby,* he will say, *put yor han
on mai bak,* because he will believe

I am really there, that his son
has been standing behind him all
these years. *Put yor hans on mai showduh,*
he will say to the cigarette smoke swirling
into the ghost of a boy, *Now flap. Yeah, lye dat, baby.*
Flap lye yu waving gootbai. See?
I telling yu . . . I telling yu. Yor daddy?
He fly.

ODYSSEUS REDUX

He entered my room like a shepherd
stepping out of a Caravaggio.

All that remains of the sentence
is a line

of black hair stranded
at my feet.

Back from the wind, he called to me
with a mouthful of crickets –

smoke & jasmine rising
from his hair. I waited

for the night to wane
into decades – before reaching

for his hands. Then we danced

without knowing it: my shadow
deepening his on the shag.

Outside, the sun kept rising.
One of its red petals fell

through the window – & caught
on his tongue. I tried

to pluck it out

               but was stopped

by my own face, the mirror,
                    its cracking, the crickets, every syllable

spilling through.

LOGOPHOBIA

Afterward, I woke
　　into the red dark
to write
　　gia dình
on this yellow pad.

Looking through the letters
　　I can see
into the earth
　　below, the blue blur
of bones.

Quickly –
　　I drill the ink
into a period.
　　The deepest hole,
where the bullet,

after piercing
　　my father's back,
has come
　　to rest.
Quickly – I climb

inside.
　　I enter
my life
　　the way words
entered me –

by falling
　　through
the silence
　　of this wide
open mouth

Ocean, don't be afraid.
The end of the road is so far ahead
it is already behind us.
Don't worry. Your father is only your father
until one of you forgets. Like how the spine
won't remember its wings
no matter how many times our knees
kiss the pavement. Ocean,
are you listening? The most beautiful part
of your body is wherever
your mother's shadow falls.
Here's the house with childhood
whittled down to a single red trip wire.
Don't worry. Just call it *horizon*
& you'll never reach it.
Here's today. Jump. I promise it's not
a lifeboat. Here's the man
whose arms are wide enough to gather
your leaving. & here the moment,
just after the lights go out, when you can still see
the faint torch between his legs.
How you use it again & again
to find your own hands.
You asked for a second chance
& are given a mouth to empty out of.
Don't be afraid, the gunfire
is only the sound of people
trying to live a little longer
& failing. Ocean. Ocean –
get up. The most beautiful part of your body
is where it's headed. & remember,
loneliness is still time spent

with the world. Here's
the room with everyone in it.
Your dead friends passing
through you like wind
through a wind chime. Here's a desk
with the gimp leg & a brick
to make it last. Yes, here's a room
so warm & blood-close,
I swear, you will wake –
& mistake these walls
for skin.

DEVOTION

Instead, the year begins
with my knees
scraping hardwood,
another man leaving
into my throat. Fresh snow
crackling on the window,
each flake a letter
from an alphabet
I've shut out for good.
Because the difference
between prayer & mercy
is how you move
the tongue. I press mine
to the navel's familiar
whorl, molasses threads
descending toward
devotion. & there's nothing
more holy than holding
a man's heartbeat between
your teeth, sharpened
with too much
air. This mouth the last
entry into January, silenced
with fresh snow crackling
on the window.
& so what – if my feathers
are burning. I
never asked for flight.
Only to feel
this fully, this
entire, the way snow
touches bare skin – & is,
suddenly, snow
no longer.

NOTES & ACKNOWLEDGEMENTS

The book's epigraph is from Bei Dao's 'Untitled', translated by Eliot Weinberger and Iona Man-Cheong.

'Threshold' borrows and alters a phrase from Carl Phillips's 'Parable'.

'Aubade with Burning City' borrows lyrics from 'White Christmas', a song written by Irving Berlin.

The epigraph for 'Immigrant Haibun' is from Edmond Jabès's *The Book of Questions*, translated by Rosemarie Waldrop.

'The Gift' is after Li-Young Lee.

The title 'Always & Forever' is also the name of my father's favorite song, as performed by Luther Vandross.

'Anaphora as Coping Mechanism' is for L.D.P.

The title 'Queen Under The Hill' is from Robert Duncan's poem 'Often I Am Permitted to Return to a Meadow'. The poem borrows and alters language from Eduardo Corral's poem 'Acquired Immune Deficiency Syndrome'.

'Notebook Fragments' borrows a phrase from Sandra Lim's 'The Dark World'; Nguyễn Chí Thiện was a Vietnamese dissident poet who spent a total of twenty-seven years in prison for his writings. While incarcerated, with no pen and paper, he composed and committed his poems to memory.

The title 'Someday I'll Love Ocean Vuong' is after Frank O'Hara and Roger Reeves.

'Devotion' is for Peter Bienkowski.

A pot of steaming jasmine tea for the editors of the publications in which some of these poems have appeared, sometimes in different forms:

The American Poetry Review, Assaracus, Beloit Poetry Journal, BODY Literature, Boston Review, Columbia Poetry Review, Court Green, Crab Orchard Review, Cream City Review, Dossier, Drunken Boat, Eleven Eleven, Gulf Coast, Linebreak, Narrative, The Nation, The New Yorker, The Normal School, PANK, Passages North, Pleiades, Poetry, Poetry Daily, Poetry Ireland, The Poetry Review, Quarterly West, South Dakota Review, Southern Indiana Review, TriQuarterly, and Verse Daily.

'Eurydice' was reprinted in *The Dead Animal Handbook* (2015); 'Ode to Masturbation' was reprinted in *Longish Poems* (2015); 'Always & Forever', 'Daily Bread', 'Prayer for the Newly Damned', and 'Self-Portrait as Exit Wounds' were reprinted in *The BreakBeat Poets* (2015); 'Deto(nation)', 'Eurydice', 'Homewrecker', and 'Telemachus' were reprinted in *Poets On Growth* (2015); 'Self-Portrait as Exit Wounds' was reprinted in *The Pushcart Prize* (2014); 'Anaphora as Coping Mechanism' was reprinted in *Best New Poets 2014*; 'Telemachus' was the winner of the 2013 Chad Walsh Prize from *Beloit Poetry Journal;* 'Prayer for the Newly Damned' was a winner of the 2012 Stanley Kunitz Prize for Younger Poets from the *American Poetry Review.*

I am grateful to the Civitella Ranieri Foundation, the Elizabeth George Foundation, the Poetry Foundation, Poets House, and the Saltonstall Foundation for the Arts, for time and support.

Thank you to Robin Robertson and Jonathan Cape for believing.

Thanks to Frances Coady for your insurmountable faith in my work.

Thank you to my dear friends, teachers and editors for helping me.

Thank you, Peter, for Peter.